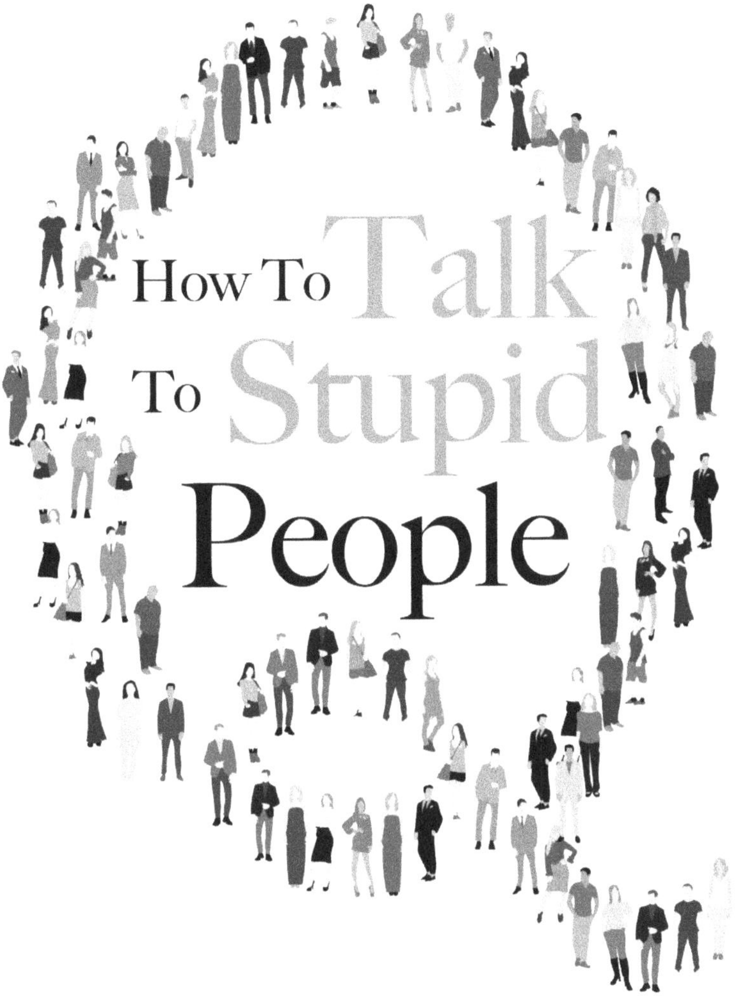

How To Talk To Stupid People

Kenneth Foard McCallion

Also by Kenneth Foard McCallion

The Marseille Connection

Saving the World One Case at a Time

Profiles in Courage in the Trump Era

Profiles in Cowardice in the Trump Era

COVID–19: The Virus that Changed America and the World

Treason & Betrayal: The Rise and Fall of Individual–1

The Essential Guide to Donald Trump

Shoreham and the Rise and Fall of the Nuclear Power Industry

For more information on these books and Kenneth, please visit www.KennethMcCallion.com

How to Talk to Stupid People

by

Kenneth Foard McCallion

Bryant Park Press

Bryant Park Press

Published by Bryant Park Press

An imprint of

Copyright © 2024 by Kenneth Foard McCallion

All rights reserved, including the right to reproduce this book or portions thereof in any form whatsoever. For information about permissions, email permissions@hhimedia.net or submit requests by facsimile to +1(203)724–0820

Cover design by Daniel Eyenegho

Book design by Christopher Klaich

Manufactured in the United States of America

Paperback ISBN: 979-8-9901199-0-1   eBook ISBN 979-8-9901199-7-0

ACKNOWLEGEMENTS

My deepest gratitude to Aaron Jerome for his invaluable contribution, without which this book would not have been possible.

DEDICATION

For my father, Harry J. McCallion, who taught us that truth matters, and that lies – when repeated often enough - can be deadly.

Chapters

Preface i
Introductory Test: Am I A Stupid Person? vii
The Dumbing Down of America 1
Why are Americans so "Agressively Ignorant"? 11
Why So Many Americans Love Cults 17
The MAGA Cult 25
How Social Media has Accelerated the "Dumbing Down" of America ... 33
How to Talk to a Trump Supporter 39
Epilogue: Making America Sane Again 43

PREFACE

Our country (and our planet) are facing numerous crises:

The **Climate Crisis** is slowly broiling us into extinction, and yet just like lobsters in a pot of hot water, where the heat is ever so slowly and imperceptibly increased, many of our compatriots remain in total denial as to what is happening to the planet. Let's call these believers in non-reality based conspiracy theories the "Flat Earthers."

The **Political Divisions** in this county are so deep and irreconcilable that the very existence of our Democracy is endangered. This has driven our country to the brink of a second Civil War. As was the case in the 1850s prelude to the First Civil War, the shooting hasn't started yet – at least as of the publication of this book anyway.

The **Opioid Crisis**, which has ravaged communities and killed tens of thousands of Americans each year since the 1980s, with no end in sight.

All of these crises—and many others I am sure you can think of—are generally well known, at least by those Americans who keep themselves reasonably well informed regarding current events and have the cognitive skills to engage in reasoned analysis and discussions regarding a wide variety of vital public issues. However, those of us who fall into this category constitute, unfortunately, a minority (yet substantial portion) of Americans.

This brings us to the **Stupidity Crisis**, arguably the most dangerous crisis that our country is facing, but which has been the subject of virtually no public discussion. Both scientific and overwhelming anecdotal evidence strongly suggests that, after a century of IQ improvement, Americans have been getting dumber. This, of course, like all generalities, does not mean that you or a family member who is part of a younger generation is less intelligent than your elders. Every generation has its share of bright and even brilliant individuals. So we are talking about averages (are you following me so far? So good. You may continue. If not, probably better to put this book down and move to the "True Romance" or comic book section of the bookstore or library).

If you are fortunate enough by some quirk of fate or intensive intellectual training to think and conduct yourself in a rational manner (not necessarily all of the time, just most of the time), then you have been confronted with the conundrum of trying to speak to your friends, neighbors or members of your family with – let's just say it – less brain power than you. They might have trouble stringing two coherent sentences together without working in a comment on how George Soros is responsible for spreading the hoax that our planet is being destroyed by a climate crisis, or that the "Deep State" is planning on mandating solar powered airliners that will be dropping from the sky if the weather turns cloudy.

For example, almost everyone has a close friend or family member who thinks that Donald J. Trump was the greatest president in history – EVER! – and that the 2020 election was deviously stolen from him by the Democrats, liberals and their sinister cabal of One-Worlders. They believe this since the ex-president himself keeps saying this, Republican leaders in Congress keep repeating this lie, and Alex Jones and other right-wing media conspiracy theorist continue to provide "new details" as to how the 2020 election was stolen. Even some previously rational and respected (if not always scrupulous) attorneys such as Rudy Giuliani "drank the cool aid" that brainwashed otherwise rational people into thinking that the 2020 election was rigged, and persisted in alleging, without any evidence, that there had been "massive voter fraud" in several key battleground states. The insurrectionists who stormed the Capitol on January 6, 2021, have been praised by Trump and his MAGA Republican cohorts as "patriots" who were just trying to tour the Capitol that day and somehow got caught up in something from which they could not extricate themselves.

Like it or not, we have now entered into a post-truth world where we are being asked to believe what some self-promoting political figure (there are many on both sides of the political spectrum) tells us to believe, rather than believing in what we can see and hear with our own eyes and ears, and with our God-given ability to reason.

No matter how you voted in the 2020 presidential election (yes, otherwise reasonable Americans actually voted for Donald J. Trump based upon an analysis that he was the "lesser of two evils"), Trump's incitement of the January 6th Capitol insurrectionists, his continued refusal to accept the results of that election, and his conviction on 34 felony counts in a Manhattan courthouse should disqualify him from earning the vote of any rational American in this 2024 election. Biden won 2020 fair and square. And yet, many of the 73 million Americans who voted for Trump in 2020 plan to vote for him again on November 5, 2024, despite the fact that his handling of the coronavirus pandemic and many other important issues during his presidential term was the political equivalent of an out-of-control dumpster fire.

So how can it be that, as I write, the 2024 presidential race is considered by the pollsters to be a close horse race? How can Kamala Harris, with Biden's strong record of accomplishments in his first term, be running neck-and-neck with a convicted felon who is a crass, crude and unabashed charlatan?

By critiquing Trump, I do not mean to suggest that all prior presidents should be given high marks for intelligence, integrity and moral rectitude. For decades there has been a raging debate among political scientists and pundits as to whether Millard Filmore or Franklin Pierce should be placed at the top of the list of the 10 worst U.S. presidents. This debate has largely been resolved with the end of Trump's tumultuous presidency. Other than die-hard Trump loyalists, there is a consensus among most knowledgeable observers that Trump is the unchallenged #1 winner of the Worst U.S. President contest.

But Trump is not solely responsible for the havoc that he wreaked on America during the four years of his presidency. We the People elected him. An American president is largely a reflection of the American people, so the election of a grossly unqualified candidate as president is a sad reflection on all of us. America's Founders such as George Washington, Thomas Jefferson, Samuel Adams, and Alexander Hamilton (to name but a few) gave us a Declaration of Independence and Constitution 240 years ago that provides us the governing principles of an imperfect yet still functioning union. American democracy has served as the model and beacon of hope for countless millions of freedom-loving people around the globe and in dozens of other countries over the span of several generations. These Founders reflected the citizenry of Colonial America and that of the early Republic, which was comprised – by and large – of hardworking, industrious and intelligent people who used their common sense and love of freedom to mount a successful revolution against the most effective military in the world, backed by the largest and perhaps most powerful empire of all time: Great Britain.

Then came a few clunkers such as Filmore and Pierce in the 1850s, whose ineptitude accelerated the country's rift into two distinct camps, inevitably leading to a great Civil War. But this crisis also gave us another great leader. By divine providence, which often seems to smile upon the United States in times of crisis despite our best efforts to tear this great democracy asunder, Abraham Lincoln emerged to lead the Union to a bloody victory over the rebel states who would not voluntarily rid themselves of the original sin of slavery and oppression of fellow human beings. What optimism he demonstrated, in ordering the continuation of the construction of the U.S. Capitol building even as the survival of the country was far from assured!

Fast forward to World War II, when the ingenuity and perseverance of the Greatest Generation of Americans, under the leadership of President Franklin Delano Roosevelt, overcame the disastrous blunders of the Harding-Coolidge-Hoover economics, and a surprise attack at Pearl Harbor to recover from the Great Depression then fight and win a two-front war simultaneously in Europe against the Nazis and in the Pacific against Imperial Japan.

Later, in the 1960s, the country rallied around the young charismatic President John F. Kennedy to beat the Russians in the space race by being the first country to put a man on the moon. America then went on to win the Cold War under the leadership of President Ronald Reagan.

After that, however, the country has – more or less – been on a downward trajectory, despite a few glimmers of brilliance. This was perhaps most visible when George W. Bush (my college classmate) and his vice president, "the Prince of Darkness" Dick Cheney, desecrated and debased the U.S. presidency by craftily spinning a treacherous web of lies and deception in order to drag America into a needless, disastrous, and costly war in Iraq.

Nevertheless, none of the recent missteps and failures by U.S. presidents could possibly approach the mendacity and contempt for democratic institutions displayed by Donald Trump during his presidency. By forming a virtual alliance with Russia's autocratic and equally megalomaniacal president, Vladimir Putin, and by making divisiveness, polarization and confrontation an acceptable political style in this country as Nixon had done decades prior, Trump deepened the already pronounced fissures in every aspect of the country's political, economic and social environment.

Indeed, he brought us to the tipping point, perhaps the point of no return, with election results being regularly challenged by losers, and voter suppression becoming a mainstream political strategy throughout the country.

But we can't blame this all on Trump. His election in 2016 was the natural and logical reflection of the downward trend in the political intelligence levels and IQs of the general population in this country over the past several decades. While a democracy can only thrive when there is a well-informed and discerning electorate that will never permit a manipulative rogue such as Trump to hold the highest office in the land, a large percentage of Americans seem to no longer have the common sense and logical capacity to prevent Trump and his ilk from taking over the reigns of power. Millions of MAGA worshippers seem willing to blindly follow the Great Orange One wherever he leads and no matter how outrageous his words and actions. As he himself famously said, he could shoot someone dead on Fifth Avenue in New York and no one would raise a finger to stop him. His Supreme Court picks seem to be working to make that a reality. And when he encouraged his mob to march on the Capitol building on January 6, 2021, his militant supporters blindly did so, engaging in outrageous acts of violence and carnage that many would not have otherwise engaged in if they had the common sense to realize the consequences of their actions.

There is now a political and social divide in this country that makes it virtually impossible for one side (let's call them the Red Team) to even speak to the other side (the Blue Team) – and visa versa - without them screaming at one another. Each side is in its own echo chamber, listening to and watching only those news programs and commentary that conform to their side's views.

This book is an attempt to help one side of the country (the Blue Team) to better understand where their family members, co-workers and neighbors who are committed to the Red Team (also sometimes referred to as "the MAGA Team") are coming from and how best to communicate with them without overt confrontation or physical injury.

INTRODUCTORY TEST: AM I A STUPID PERSON?

This is an "honor system" test, with no use of Google or the internet permitted. The answers will be provided in the sequel to this book, which has the working title *Answers to the Most Frequently Asked Questions About Stupid People* (suggested price: $17.95; projected release date: June 2028; complimentary tee-shirt "How to Talk to Stupid People" comes with each purchase of book).

1. **Who won the 2020 presidential election?**

   a) Joe Biden

   b) Donald Trump, by a landslide, but it was stolen from him.

   c) Don't know.

2. **Should the U.S. Spend billions of dollars completing the building of a wall on its southern border to protect it from illegal immigration, even though those who want to enter the U.S. Illegally have found little difficulty circumventing it?**

   a) Yes. We should always finish what we start, no matter how ridiculous the idea or how effective it is.

   b) No.

   c) Not sure, but maybe it's worth a try.

3. **If you answered "yes" to question #2, do you think that the wall will stop people from coming legally into the country by flying in with visas and then overstaying their visas?**

   a) Yes, definitely.

   b) No.

   c) It depends on how high the Wall is.

4. The southern border of the U.S. separates the U.S from what country?
   a) Canada
   b) Cuba
   c) Gulf of Mexico
   d) Mexico

5. What country does the U.S. Border to its north?
   a) Greenland
   b) Iceland
   c) Canada
   d) Alaska

6. What was the color of napoleon's white horse?
   a) White
   b) Don't know.

7. Who is buried in grant's tomb?
   a) General Ulysses S. Grant
   b) General Grant and his wife
   c) Land Grant
   d) None of the above

8. Vice President Kamala Harris should be required to "prove" that she and President Biden won the 2020 presidential election before she is permitted to continue to run for the presidency in the 2024 election.
   a) Yes, definitely.
   b) No.
   c) The Republican-dominated Supreme Court should decide who wins a close presidential election, just as it did in the 2000 election between Bush and Gore.

Introductory Test · ix

9. **Biden won 80 million votes in the 2020 presidential election because there was massive voter fraud throughout the country.**

   a) Yes, definitely.

   b) No.

10. **What is the electoral college?**

    a) A school of higher education that can be found in every state, which is financed as part of the state budget by state legislatures and by land grants.

    b) A vestigial political organ that somehow found its way into the U.S. Constitution in 1789 as a last line of defense against a corrupt person unduly influenced by a hostile foreign power from being elected to the U.S. Presidency, but which recent events have shown does not work and should be discarded as soon as possible.

    c) A state party school that is financed by lucrative T.V. contracts for its football, basketball and/or beach volleyball programs.

11. **What is a vestigial organ?**

    a) An organ that may have once served a purpose for our ancestors long ago - such as the appendix, coccyx (tailbone), or wisdom teeth, but will not be missed if removed.

    b) A musical instrument, often found in churches.

    c) None of the above.

12. **Do you have to wear pants during a zoom conference?**

    a) No, the camera on your computer can only "see" the upper part of your body.

    b) Yes, since you can never be sure if the camera on your computer is on "hold" or not when you stand up.

    c) What is a Zoom conference?

13. **Why do North and South Dakota, who together have a population of less than one million people, collectively have four senators in congress, while California, with over more than 40 million people, has only two senators?**

    a) The people of North and South Dakota are better negotiators and struck a better deal when they became states.

    b) Article 1 of the U.S. Constitution has a typographical error in it providing that each state, no matter how large or small, more populous or not, gets two Senators each, no matter how unfair that may seem.

    c) The Founders who drafted the U.S. Constitution in 1789 reached a compromise between larger, more populous states, and smaller and less populous states, where the number of each state's representatives to Congress in the House of Representatives would be based on the populations of each state, while each state would get two senators in the other legislative body of Congress: the Senate. (This may or may not have had something to do with preserving the power of states where enslaved people were not considered as "counting" towards state population).

    d) North and South Dakota were not states when the U.S. Constitution was passed, so they should not have four votes in the U.S. Senate.

14. **Is Puerto Rico a part of the U.S.?**

    a) Yes, but it is a territory, not a state.

    b) No, it is an independent country.

    c) Not sure.

15. **What is the primary language spoken by the residents of Puerto Rico?**

    a) English

    b) Spanish

    c) Spanglish

16. **Should puerto rico be admitted as a state?**
    a) No, you must be kidding.
    b) No, but they should only be allowed to have non-voting "observers" in the House of Representatives and in the Senate.
    c) Yes, the Commonwealth of Puerto Rico has been an "unincorporated territory" of the U.S. since 1898 and it's admission to statehood is long overdue.

17. **What is puerto rico's major export?**
    a) Ricky Martin.
    b) Rum.
    c) Pharmaceuticals and medical equipment.
    d) Salsa.

18. **Are rapid-fire assault weapons protected by the second amendment?**
    a) Yes, of course. That is exactly what the Founders must have had in mind. No matter that the Sandy Hook shooter fired 155 rounds within a matter of a few minutes, killing 20 students and 6 adults.
    b) Absolutely not.

19. **Can "Jesus," Pope John Paul II or other historical figure really be one of your facebook "friends?"**
    a) Yes, of course. Jesus is one of my BFFs on Facebook. What's wrong with that?
    b) Are you kidding?
    c) Not sure.

20. **If you were assigned as a crew member on a space mission to the sun, when would be the best time to go there?**
    a) At Night. It is too hot during the day.
    b) No time would be "best." The temperature of the sun is always too hot.
    c) I'd ask for another mission.

21. The earth revolves around what object in the solar system?

   a) The moon.

   b) The sun.

   c) Donald J. Trump.

   d) Trick question. The earth does not move.

Next step: if you feel good about most or all of your answers, proceed to chapter one.

Chapter 1
The Dumbing Down of America

Have you ever had the feeling that people have been getting dumber and harder to talk to? If so, you are not alone. When asked which direction human intelligence is headed, most people say that it is on the decline.

So, does that mean we are headed for a society controlled by idiots? The 2006 film "Idiocracy" portrayed this scenario, with the opening scenes showing Army Private Joe Bowers (actor Luke Wilson) being selected to take part in a secret military experiment to put him in hibernation for a year along with a woman named Rita (actor Maya Rudolph). However, when the facility the two are being stored in is closed down, they remain forgotten until 2505, when they finally wake up. To their amazement, they find that human intelligence has dramatically declined in the interim, and that Joe is now the smartest person in the world. Most people stay at home with their headphones on, fixated to one or more screens that provide them with an endless stream of entertaining nonsense. Speech has devolved to the point where it only consists of a few ridiculous phrases of text speak. Worst of all, famine is looming after farmers began watering their crops with a Gatorade-like sports drink.

The prevailing intuitive sense that we are experiencing a serious dumbing down of our society is also supported by the trend in standardized testing since the 1970s. During the first seven decades of the 20th Century, IQ tests showed an increase of about 3 IQ points per decade, at least up until the 1970s. This was known as the "Flynn effect," first described in the 1980s by researcher James Flynn, who studied trends in IQ test scores up until that time.[1] There were several theories that were developed to explain this phenomenon. One explanation was that improvements in health and nutrition were responsible, including a decrease in smoking and alcohol use during pregnancy, the discontinuation of the use of

---

1   The Flynn Effect: A Meta-analysis - PMC - PubMed Central (PMC)www.ncbi.nlm.nih.gov/pmc/articles/PMC4152423/

harmful lead paint, and improvements in the prevention and treatment of infectious diseases.

But then, for some reason, human intelligence started to decline, as confirmed by standardized testing. For example, when scientists from the Norway's Ragnar Frisch Centre for Economic Research analyzed 730,000 IQ tests given to Norwegian men before their compulsory military service from 1970 to 2009, they found that average IQ scores were actually dropping. And they were dropping by a lot![2] Each generation of Norwegian men appeared to be getting around seven IQ points dumber.

Now, you may be saying to yourself: Why do I care if Norwegians are getting dumber? I am not a Norwegian, I am American (or Canadian, Mexican, whatever). However, there is strong evidence from other studies that the drop in Norwegian IQ scores has been consistent with a downward trend in intelligence everywhere on the planet. Research published in June 2018 in Proceedings of the U.S. National Academy of the Sciences examined the IQ scores of men born between 1962 and 1991.[3] Researchers found that scores increased for men born between 1962 and 1975. However, they decreased steadily among men born after 1975.

Not only were people (or at least men) getting dumber as time went on, but studies also showed that the stronger the opinions that were held by the people being studied, the less likely that their beliefs and opinions were based on verified objective knowledge or scientific understanding. Conversely, the more reliable the information that people had on a subject, the less likely they were to hold extreme and intransigent views.[4] For example, the more extreme the views of opponents of genetically modified foods, the less they actually knew about the subject. Similarly, in a study involving opinions regarding the application of genetic engineering technology (gene therapy), those people who were the more outspoken and extreme in the opposition to the use of gene therapy, tended to know less about the workings and understood risks of gene therapy.

As a result, the global trend has been towards dumber and less informed people confidently expressing the most extreme views, unsupported

---

2 Oslo's Ragnar Frisch Center for Economic Research Norwegian Study: IQ Scores Dropped for Decades - VOA, learningenglish.voanews.com/a/norwegian-study-iq-scores-dropped-for-decades

3 Study: People Are Getting Dumber | National News | US NewsStudy: People Are Getting Dumber | National News | US News June 14, 2018

4 Extreme opponents of genetically modified foods know the least but think they know the most | Nature Human Behaviour

by objective facts or scientific analysis. On top of this natural human tendency towards overconfident idiocy, we have the internet enabling "information" to spread faster than ever before, and social media recommendation algorithms prioritizing inflammatory, extreme content. None of this bodes well for the human species, nor the planet which we are supposed to be protecting as its stewards. As an example, on February 26, 2015, Oklahoma Sen. Jim Inhofe brought a snowball to the Senate floor during a debate on climate change, holding the melting snowball in his outstretched arm, and declaring that it was "proof" that climate change was a hoax.[5] Although 99.9% of the world's scientists now believe that climate change is a reality, not just a theory, 40% of the U.S. population think that human-induced climate change is a hoax.[6] 16% of the U.S. population believe the earth is flat.[7] Trump himself added to this climate crisis denialism by declaring during a Fox News interview that climate change was "a hoax."[8]

Scientist are puzzled by this "dumber but more opinionated" phenomenon. Some blame the terrible diets of most Americans;[9] others blame our tech obsession;[10] and still others blame the media for giving people whatever they want to hear, whether or not it is true.[11] Cornell psychologists David Dunning and Justin Kruger studied this phenomenon and first described it in a 1999 paper titled "Unskilled and unaware of it: how difficulties in recognizing one's own incompetence lead to inflated self-assessments." The "Dunning-Kruger effect," as it is now widely known, is a cognitive bias that causes people to overestimate their abilities or knowledge, even when they lack expertise in a particular area. This effect – which is particularly prevalent among gun owners - can lead to poor decision-making and highly dangerous situations, such as when a father gives his teenage son - who has been generating threatening and hate-filled text messages – a gun as a present, and the gun is then used

---

5   https://www.cbsnews.com/news/sen-jim-inhofe...
6   The Print, Trump's America has the most number of flat earth believers & climate change deniers, GARETH DORRIAN and IAN WHITTAKER, 26 May, 2018.
7   Id.
8   On Fox, Donald Trump Calls Climate Change A 'Hoax': 'In ... - Forbes https://www.forbes.com/sites/markjoyella/2022/03/...
9   www.psychologytoday.com/us/blog/bad-appetite/200910/hey-stupid-how-your-e...
10 Is Technology Making Us Dumber? | Psychology Today https://www.psychologytoday.com/.../200911/is-technology-making-us-dumber
11 Social Media Is Making Us Dumber. Here's Exhibit A. https://www.nytimes.com/2018/01/11/opinion/social...

by the teenager to kill two teachers and two students at his local high school on the first day of the school year.

One thing that we know is not causing this trend is the eugenic theory that dumber people have more kids and are therefore increasing their percentage share of the 7.5 billion people on the planet.[12] This "dumbing down" of society has been even further accelerated by the continuing drop in IQ scores. When you analyze the IQ scores of brothers who were born in different years, which you would expect to be similar because of genetics, the brothers' IQ scores were often significantly different, with younger brother born in the 1970s or thereafter having consistently lower scores than their older siblings.[13]

Some of this "dumbing down" may be due to "political correctness" or economics, or a combination of both. Based on the generally altruistic impulse to not want to make people with lower intelligence feel "left out," many of our educational and cultural institutions have been watered down. Even worse, our mass media has "dumbed down" virtually every aspect of our entertainment and news, including our language, so that everything is as simple and as uncomplicated as possible. This means that our vocabularies and conceptual references are more limited. While prior generations worked hard to use as wide a range of words and language as possible, the trend now – especially when texting is involved – is to keep things as simple and uncomplicated as possible, even at the cost of incorrect spelling of words. Websites are "optimized" to the average reading levels of 10 to 13 year olds. Conversations in person or in the media avoid being too "highbrow" or "intellectual" or "abstract," in favor of short soundbites that are so simple minded that they used to be reserved for pro-wresting commentary, but have now become universal.

One of the likely reasons why former President Trump is such an "effective" communicator is that he has the most limited vocabulary and uses the fewest number of words than any preceding president.[14] He also avoided figures of speech, such as similes and metaphors, which require higher levels of cognitive processing.

When Trump first started talking about the need to build a wall to keep immigrants from illegally entering the country, many people

---

12   Study: People Are Getting Dumber - US News & World Report
https://www.usnews.com/news/national-news/articles/...
13   iq-brain.com/iq-differences-between-siblings/
14   https://www.newsweek.com/trump-fire-and-fury-smart-genius-obama-774169

– including this author – thought that he could not possibly be talking about a *literal* physical wall that would cost billions of dollars and cover thousands of miles, and would probably not be very effective in keeping people from crossing the border if they were really motivated to do so. Rather, I thought that he was speaking metaphorically about tightening up procedures at border crossings and at airports, as well as restricting the movements of migrant and seasonal workers crossing the southern border.

I was wrong. Trump was, in fact, talking about a physical wall, even though statistics clearly showed that most illegal immigrants had legally entered the country at airports, with legal visas, and then overstayed their visa time periods, thus becoming illegal. Trump must have known this, but talking about "immigration reform" can quickly get complicated and boring, and one's eyes inevitably tend to glaze over after a while.

Trump's genius is that he is able to—or perhaps only able to—dumb issues down to their most basic level, Even if his policies may be basically ridiculous and ineffective, they are easily understandable. Everyone knows what a wall is, and when Trump declared that the way to solve complex immigration problems was to build a "big beautiful wall" that Mexico would pay for, it had elegance of simplicity, even if upon closer analysis (which Trump avoided at all costs) it was non-sensical and fundamentally dishonest. Economist and blogger Tyler Cowen suggests that this "dumbing down" of political discourse is creating a more "stupidity-inducing environment."

Our tech obsession (some might say domination) may have something to do with it, but this cannot be all of the answer, since IQ scores started dropping in the 1970s, long before the tech revolution really took off and people started staring at screens all day.

Other possible explanations are the prevalence of unhealthy, fast-food diets, trashy media, and the decline (or near-death experience) of reading, at least the reading of books. My personal favorite theory is that our brains are gradually rotting from microplastics and the chemical saturating our junk food, lack of exercise, obesity and diabetes in epidemic proportions, as well as from the unhealthy light waves emanating from our computer screens and iPhones.

* * *

Which brings us inevitably to the U.S. presidential election of 2020. If ever there was a moment of truth that our country is facing a "stupidity crisis" of monumental proportion, the events that transpired between election day, November 3, 2020 and January 20, 2021 (spoiler alert: the date that Joe Biden and Kamala Harris were sworn in as President and Vice President), should dispel any doubts that we have a serious "intelligence deficit" in this country.

O.K. I get it that we had a coronavirus pandemic that is raging out of control, and that we had an economic crisis, food anxiety crisis and a collective national mental health crisis, all of which had to be addressed at the same time. But we also have an epidemic of stupidity facing the country, which is as serious as the crystal meth, fentanyl, heroin and other epidemics that we heard about so much just a year or two ago, but not much since. I didn't hear any news that those crises were solved, since I basically stopped watching T.V. during the Covid pandemic.

Don't get the false impression that I don't care about what is happening out there in our country. I do. I used to be a news junky, until my doctor suggested that sitting at home and shouting at the T.V. during the first few months of the pandemic lockdown wasn't the healthiest thing for me. So I did follow the election results on November 3, 2020 and for a few days after that, when most of the networks (other than Fox News) slowly and cautiously declared Biden the winner. My thinking was that if Fox was the first to declare Biden the winner in Arizona, and then as the winner in the electoral college votes, that was good enough for me. After all, Fox News is practically the official news channel for Trump and all things Republican, so if they were calling it for Biden, who was I to disagree?

I tuned in once again on January 6, 2021, since things were kind of slow in the New Year and I thought it would be interesting to see the important, but rather dull, formality of watching Vice President Mike Pence count the electoral votes in the Senate and formally declare Biden as the winner. I had last watched this largely ceremonial event on January 5, 2001, when Vice President Al Gore, acting as President of the Senate, declared George W. Bush the victor in an election that had been (in my view and that of a few others) had been "stolen" from Gore. The U.S. Supreme Court, in a party-line 5-4 vote in *Bush v. Gore*, ordered a stop to the partial recount going on there that was ordered by the Florida Supreme Court, thus effectively delivering the White House to Bush without proper knowledge of the actual final vote tally. I remember Gore shutting down some rather irate Democratic members of Congress (and many non-members, including me) who were hopping mad over this. What a great country, I thought, where the winner of the popular vote in a national election could so graciously concede to the loser in the popular vote (by a lot), just because his opponent had won by a razor-thin margin in the Electoral College. However, this majority of the ballots in the Electoral College could only have come about when the Supreme Court put its collective finger on the scales and delivered enough Florida electoral votes to Bush to push him over the top.

Even though, in my view and that of countless others, Al Gore and the American people had been robbed blind by the Supreme Court's politically-partisan based decision, Gore's concession prioritized the seamless and harmonious transfer of power, despite the fundamental unfairness that brought about that result.

Fast forward to January 6, 2021, where all of the cable channels were live broadcasting the "Save America" rally that the outgoing president, Donald J. Trump, was holding near the White House. It looked like there were at hundreds, at most a few thousand, people with red MAGA hats and Trump flags, not very different than the T.V. images of Trump's many rallies, where the crowd gets fired up, enjoying the show that Trump never failed to deliver on, and then went home feeling good about themselves and with their faith renewed in their Supreme Leader. He had promised them a Great Big Beautiful Wall on the Southern Border to keep the hordes of bloodthirsty and dangerous Hispanics massing to our south, and he promised that Americans wouldn't even have to pay for it. Although not much of the Wall actually got built and Mexico never paid for it, this was really not Trump's fault (in the view of the MAGA faithful), since the shadowy cabal of Democrats, "deep staters," child-eating pedophiles and the demonic puppet master himself, George Soros, thwarted Trump at every turn.

Then Trump labelled his mob "patriots" and called on them to march down Pennsylvania Avenue to the U.S. Capitol and stop Mike Pence and Congress from doing whatever they were doing, which clearly in Trump's view was nothing good. "You'll never take back our country with weakness," Trump exhorted the crowd. "You have to show strength, and you have to be strong," he told his followers. "Fight like hell!" he gasped.

I was clearly puzzled. What was he expecting the crowd to do once they marched down to the Capitol? Protesting outside of Congress wasn't going to change anything, if all that Congress was doing was just counting the electoral slates sent to it by the states? Then the TV commentators explained for people like me who had been out of the "loop" or visiting distant planets, that Trump still thought that he had won the election "by a landslide," and that he thought the election had been "stolen" from him through "massive voter fraud." The commentators went to great lengths to point out that Trump was "lying" and that every election official and about 60 judges had already found that Team Trump had failed to come forward with any significant evidence of massive voter fraud that would have changed the election results in any of the key battleground states.

Then a lawyer, Rudy Giuliani, took the stage and, with Trump approvingly watching, told the increasingly agitated crowd that, in essence, the only way they could save their country and their democracy was through "trial by combat." If those were not fighting words, then I don't know what is. But Trump did not unleash the crowd yet. A Congressman from Georgia by the name of Mo Brooks raised the level of anger and aggrievement of the crowd several more degrees by telling them that they should "kick some ass," obviously referring to the miscreants in Congress who seemed to be poised to certify the election in Biden's favor for no other good reason that he won the most electoral votes. If the president was saying that Biden had stolen the election, then it must be true. After all, he was their president and commander-in-chief, and if you can't believe him, who can you believe?

It must have looked awfully suspicious that it took the Republican Senate Majority Leader Mitch McConnell six weeks after election day to acknowledge that Biden had won the election. How complicated can it be? The voters vote. Then the poll workers and election officials count the ballots and report the results to the Secretary of State, state legislators and governors of each state. Then the slate of electors for the candidate who won in that state is forwarded to Congress to be counted on January 6. If it took someone as smart as Mitch McConnell six weeks to be able to come out and say that Biden had won (and Trump had lost) there must be something genuinely fishy about the election, especially since the president and two of the really smart senators – Ted Cruz and Josh Hawley - were still saying that it had been stolen from Trump.

Both Senator Ted Cruz from Texas, and Senator Josh Hawley of Missouri, had clerked for U.S. Supreme Court justices, which is in all earnestness a really big deal. It means that they must have done very well in college and law school, and were two of the best and brightest that this country has to offer. And yet they were still disputing the results of the election and calling for an Election Commission to investigate the election results in several states. The last time this had happened was in 1876, when the Republicans and Democrats had each submitted competing slates of electors to Congress for the states of Georgia, Florida and Louisiana. An Election Commission was formed, but before it could get underway, the two parties cut a deal whereby the Democrats agreed not to contest the election of Rutherford B. Hayes of Ohio as the next President. But the Republicans had to agree to withdraw federal troops from these states, so that they could go back to the way things were before the Civil War, with blacks being denied the right to vote and to exercise many of the other rights of U.S. citizenship. With "Jim Crow" laws quickly enacted in Southern states, institutionalized segregation became the law once again throughout the South. This was the legacy of America's last disputed election.

Needless to say, the Biden team was less than thrilled at the Republican proposal of another Election Commission, especially since there were no states where the election results were in serious dispute, and the state legislators and governors were in agreement as to who had won the election in their disputed states: Joe Biden. President Trump probably wasn't too crazy about this Election Commission idea anyway, since there was always a danger that, in the end, they would still declare Biden the winner, which was not an option that Trump wanted on the table. It would be much easier for Mike Pence and the Congress to just invalidate enough Biden electors to swing the election to Trump, and then declare him the winner. Why didn't Pence and the Republican majority in the Senate understand how easy it would be to just flip the election results?

Trump finally realized that if his allies in the U.S. Capitol did not have the guts to pull off this coup, then he would have to do it the hard way. He launched his massed troops on an unsuspecting and unprepared Capitol building, and they soon overran the sparce defenses.

Some of the Trump supporters were full-fledged domestic terrorists who stormed the Capitol, beat police officers (killing one of them), and stalked the halls of Congress shouting, "Hang Mike Pence" and "Kill Pelosi." Their intent was to interrupt the Congressional proceedings, hold members of Congress and the Vice President hostage, and possibly kill them. They were insurrectionist. And while very few if any of them were arrested that fateful day, many of them were tracked down later on and prosecuted for their crimes against the United States and its citizens.

However, it seems fairly clear that there were some others in the mob that attacked the Capitol who were carried along with the crowd. They wandered around the Capitol for a while, taking some photos and selfies to send back home to their friends, and were not there to overthrow the government, or to take hostage and kill elected officials. Rather, they were just acting stupidly, and although they should have known better, they didn't. This doesn't mean that they should be legally let off the hook and given a free pass for illegally trespassing in the Capitol. They should be held responsible for their crimes and should pay a penalty, but it should also be taken into account at sentencing that they are members of the Trump cult and were following the directions of the then sitting president of the United States.

Chapter 2
WHY ARE AMERICANS SO "AGGRESSIVELY IGNORANT"?

The downward trajectory of American's IQ scores is compounded by the fact that many Americans pride themselves on their ignorance and are deeply suspicious of their more educated and better-informed fellow citizens. This toxic combination of low intelligence and "aggressive ignorance" makes Americans even more susceptible to the simplistic answers to complex questions and the false conspiracy theories being offered by various cults, including the Trump MAGA movement. It is much easier to demonize asylum seekers crossing the southern U.S. border as "rapists" and "murderers" who could be successfully barred from entering the country by a Wall, than it is to formulate a fair but effective immigration plan. The former requires no thought process whatsoever, which makes it so attractive to so many.

Many prominent people who come from abroad but have chosen to make America their home have remarked on the stark contrast between America and most of the rest of the world when it comes to issues of education, applied intelligence, and work ethic. For example, Elon Musk, who was born in Pretoria, South Africa, and grew up in Canada, has candidly expressed his view that the Chinese and others in many foreign countries are much smarter and hardworking than Americans. "The sheer number of really smart, hardworking people in China is incredible," Musk said during a 2023 interview with podcaster Lex Fridman. "How many smart, hardworking people are there in China? There's far more of them there than there are here, I think, in my opinion, and they've got a lot of energy." Musk added: "The architecture in China that's in recent years is far more impressive than the U.S. I mean the train stations, the buildings, the high-speed rail, everything, it's really far more impressive than what we have in the U.S.," adding, "I recommend somebody just go to Shanghai and Beijing, look at the buildings, and go take the train from Beijing to Xi'An, where you have the terracotta warriors."

Without a doubt, over the past few decades, China has successfully concluded numerous ambitious projects, including the construction of the world's largest high-speed rail network, extensive modern highways, and countless bridges, including some of the longest in the world. By comparison, many U.S. airports are older and in worse shape than those in many third world or emerging countries. It is a disgrace, in a country that used to be the leader in world technology, innovation and infrastructure development. Many of our key jobs in American industry are filled by H1B visa holders, since they are foreigners with unique skills who are critical to our country's economic development (and survival) because there are no available natural-born Americans with these required skills. Granted, one would expect there to be "more" clever people in China than in the US, given that China's population is over four times larger.

Going deeper than Musk's generalizations, historian Richard Hofstadter produced two remarkable works on the role of what I'd like to call American idiocy. In *Anti-Intellectualism in American Life* (1963) and *The Paranoid Style in American Politics* (1964), Hofstadter drew a connection between American beliefs in self-sufficiency and the equality of members of the community on the one hand, and a deep distrust of expertise and established authorities on the other. The fundamental focus on freedom, hard work, and equality of people meant that any expert was either an egghead or the crony of some shadowy, manipulative foreign power seeking to destroy the American way of life. These strains of thought remain apparent in the US political system today, where climate denialism is often complemented with a belief that owning a pick-up truck is the definition of freedom. Hofstadter did, however, see a silver-lining in these tendencies which also produced a deep-seated resistance of authoritarian government—at least when the relatively wealthy and politically empowered come see government initiatives as intruding in their lives. Nevertheless, as the world grows ever-more complex, any salutary effects of American idiocy are likely to dissipate.

Here are some of the factors that – totally apart from a lack of raw intelligence and brain power- place America at a severe disadvantage on the world stage:

1. Poor Geography Skills

Many Americans struggle to locate even large countries on a world map. Many more cannot even identify all 50 U.S. states correctly (or even a few). This lack of basic geography knowledge makes us seem ignorant to others about the world beyond our borders – and they would be correct. The Atlantic and Pacific have long guarded America from invasion and war, but they've also isolated and constrained American thinking about our place in the wider world.

To people from other countries who learn world geography in school and understand the ever increasing importance of geography in an interconnected world, our basic ignorance about where places and countries are located seems incomprehensible.

2. Limited Foreign Language Skills

Most Americans only speak English, except for the large minority that speaks Spanish or another language, usually because it is their native tongue. Maintaining bilingual homes usually, however, fades after a few generations in the U.S. This is in sharp contrast with other countries, where it is common for people to speak multiple languages, with English usually being one of them. Our reluctance or inability to learn other languages places most Americans at an even greater disadvantage than mere lack of intelligence or limited knowledge.

3. Limited Knowledge of World Events

Many Americans don't even try keep up with news and events happening outside the U.S., and the same applies to newsworthy events within the U.S. as well. A lack of widespread world-history education about foreign cultures and lands has compounding effects throughout life, as most Americans never meaningfully engage with the world beyond U.S. borders. This lack of awareness about global – or even national - issues compounds the well-deserved reputation of most Americans as self-centered and, yes, basically ignorant.

When we can't participate knowledgeably in discussions of important national and world events, it makes us even more susceptible to false prophets and charismatic charlatans who are more than willing to provide us with easy answers and a simplistic world view, no matter how false it may be.

4. Unhealthy Eating Habits

The American diet, which is dominated by fast food, microwave meals and other unhealthy options, has led not only to an epidemic in obesity and weigh-related illnesses, such as diabetes, but to the dangerous yet "politically correct" notion that "fat shaming" and every mild criticism of unhealthy American eating habits cannot be tolerated. This makes us appear to be among the unhealthiest people on the planet, which would be correct. Ultra-processed foods make up over 50% of the average American's diet, contributing not only to physical diseases, but also to mental health issues. Higher consumption of ultra-processed foods (like sodas, chicken nuggets, and chips) also harms brain development in children, is associated with decreased cognitive function in adults, and is linked to depression and generally feeling worse about yourself.[1]

Our obesity rates and reliance on "fast" processed foods not only jeopardizes our health, but it also contributes to our susceptibility to "fast" ideas and easy answers to even the most complex questions.

5. Overconfidence Despite Ignorance

American "exceptionalism" has always been a core American belief since the birth of our nation. We have always viewed our country as somehow better than others, with a destiny protected by divine providence. After all, we are the birthplace of modern democracy, and our economy and seemingly endless opportunities for advancement have been the envy of the world for more than a century. But this "American dream" has become tarnished. While it has not quite devolved into the "American carnage" nightmare that Donald Trump would have us believe, there can be little doubt that America is no longer the land of opportunity as it was viewed just a generation or two ago, when it was believed that with hard work and dedication, anything was possible, and that every new generation would have a better life than the last.

Instead, America is viewed by many as a "has been" country, with the Chinese development model and a deeply united European Union being

---

1 https://www.sciencefocus.com/the-human-body/processed-food-impact-brain

perceived by many as having much more to offer in terms of development opportunity and upward mobility. Indeed, many of us have seen our friends and work colleagues who have some family or other ties to Europe or Scandinavia turning their back on America for what they perceive as better opportunities and a better way of life for themselves and their families by leaving the United States – which is a deeply divided, fundamentally violent and gun-loving country perpetually on brink of a Second Civil War.

And yet most Americans are clueless about the perilous realities and dangers faced by their country, and instead, still deserve the stereotype of "the Ugly American" that has dogged us for decades, as being loudly opinionated about topics they know little about. This combination of strong opinions and lack of knowledge displays an arrogance that has led to a dysfunctional political and institutional landscape.

6. Bizarre Public Rituals

The very-public White House presidential "pardon" of a turkey each year at Thanksgiving strikes many non-Americans as mystifying and non-sensical. What about the other countless thousands of turkeys slaughtered each year in anticipation of turkey dinners across the country? What was their "crime" which led to their capital punishment and execution? And for the turkey (or turkeys) spared this barbaric annual ritual of death and dismemberment and "pardoned," what was so special about them? We are never told.

And then there is the quaint American tradition of Groundhog Day, celebrated every year on February 2 at Punxsutawney, Pennsylvania. According to superstition, if the groundhog emerges from its burrow on this day and sees its shadow, it will retreat to its den and winter will go on for six more weeks. If it does not see its shadow, Spring will arrive early. Americans persist in this annual ritual despite the fact that meteorological studies have conclusively shown that there is absolutely no correlation between the groundhog sighting of its own shadow and the arrival of Spring. And how do people know anyway whether it sees its own shadow or not, or whether the groundhog is just terrified of the many mindless reporters surrounding it shooting off flashbulbs in its face?

7. Believing Weird Conspiracy Theories

As discussed more fully in the next chapter, many Americans believe in far-fetched conspiracy theories that seem ridiculous to people in other countries. From beliefs that the Earth is flat, to QAnon, to "aggressively ignorant" MAGA believers who believe that Trump can do no wrong and ignore any facts that would get in the way of their unchallengeable faith in the Great Orange One, Americans look simple-minded, gullible and out of touch with reality to non-Americans—especially when it comes to religion and politics. Our willingness to spread these theories online and to uncritically accept whatever wild disinformation campaign is being dished out by hostile sources such as Russia, China or North Korea makes us the laughingstock of the rest of the world, and, more importantly, puts our entire political and democratic system of government on the brink of collapse.

Chapter 3
WHY SO MANY AMERICANS LOVE CULTS

America is not the only nation on the planet that has cults, but the sheer abundance of American cults and the eagerness of so many Americans to embrace the most outlandish of conspiracy theories and fake news promoted by various cult leaders is a phenomenon that is hard to explain. In a country which traditionally embraced rugged individualism, taking pride in our ability to use our reasoning ability and experience to make important life decisions for ourselves, how did it come about that cult membership – where you willingly sacrifice your own intellectual independence for a total submission to a set of beliefs formulated by someone else - became so attractive to so many Americans? Here are some of the possible reasons:

Cults tend to attract people with limited intelligence.

Everyone struggles with coping in a complex world where they have been required to make their own decisions and to live with the consequences of the bad ones they have made. People with lower levels of intelligence struggle even harder. Relying on external authority figures and a tight-knit community allows people to shrug off their feelings of personal responsibility and self-doubt.

Cults promote an illusion of comfort and group "belonging".

Humans desire comfort, and in a fearful and uncertain world, cults provide the illusion of comfort. Cult leaders often make promises that are, realistically speaking, totally unattainable but nonetheless tantalizing, since they reflect the deepest of human desires. Cult promises may include moral purity, financial security, total health, constant peace of mind, and even eternal life.

Cults satisfy the human desire for absolute answers.

We are confronted every day with complex issues and problems, very few of which have clear black-and-white answers. We are surrounded by ambiguity and abstractions, and we are often unsure which way to turn. But the human brain is not wired to work that way most of the time. Humans crave clarity and certainty, which is what is offered by cults. They offer solid, absolute answers for fundamental questions such as identifying good vs. evil, the meaning of life, what set of political beliefs is good for the country, etc. Cult leaders promote messages that are simple—a comforting, if illusory, alternative to what real life has to offer. New members are promised a simple life that does not require them to make life decisions; these decisions have already been made by the cult leader, who supposedly has it all figured out.

Cults attract people with low self-esteem, which makes them more likely to be persuaded by a cult environment.

People with low self-esteem are easier to break down psychologically, then build back up in an effort to teach them that the cult is the supportive environment they're looking for. Those that lack confidence and self-esteem are far more likely to fall for a pyramid scheme that promises a better life, with all the important decisions made by the self-assured, all-knowing cult leader.

Cults often "love bomb" their new recruits.

The phrase "love bombing" is often used by cult insiders to describe the ways in which someone with low self-esteem is consistently flattered, complimented, and seduced into associating the cult with love and acceptance. When someone feels unworthy of love, they are the first to fall for the false flatteries associated with love bombing. This often leads to overly intense, unhealthy, and inappropriate levels of closeness and "love" which often develops when the weak and preyed upon and exploited.

What goes up, must, of course, come down. Initial periods of love-bombing are typically followed by targeted degrading language and behavior whenever cultists slightly misstep. This encourages complete obedience, which is rewarded with over the top praise. This cycle of emotional conditioning all-to-often leads to sexual abuse, child marriage, child abuse, and sex trafficking, the tragic outcomes of cult membership.

Women are more likely than men to join a cult.

While defining what exactly constitutes a "cult" is notoriously slippery, most cult researchers have found that women are more susceptible than men to joining.[1] The reasons for this are not fully known. One theory is that since women have been oppressed for much of human history, they are programmed to be drawn to counter-cultural alternative sources of belief and authority figures. Another theory is that young women are often taught to seek the attention of men, which is most certainly being offered by male cult leaders, who frequently channel spiritualism to sexually exploit their followers. It may also be the simple fact that it's more likely for a woman to join a cult when she is greeted by other women who are a part of the group. Women tend to feel safe around other women.

Cult Leaders Are Masters of Mind Control.

Cult leaders repeat various lies and distortions until members find it difficult to distinguish between reality and the lies that they are being constantly told. A strong dose of paranoia is also interjected into the cult teachings, creating an "Us" against "Them" siege mentality. Cult leaders often preach to their faithful that the government, the United Nations, the "deep state," the worldwide Jewish-Leftist conspiracy, the papists, and other shadowy, powerful groups are out to get them, and that they must not listen to the mainstream, which is constantly spewing "fake news" and lies.

---

1   https://www.damemagazine.com/2021/07/19/are-women-more-susceptible-to-cults/

Many cult members have tried and rejected Organized Religion.

Many people who join cults have experienced mainstream religions at some point in their lives, before going on to rejected them. Many cults provide a feeling of fulfilment for the fundamental human longing for answers to the mysteries of life, by giving the cult members a quasi-religious experience, complete with absolute answers and complete certainties.

The Seekers

One of the most notable studies into cult dynamics was by U.S. psychologist Leon Festinger and his colleagues, who published a book in 1956 entitled *When Prophecy Fails*.

It documented the case of a group called "The Seekers" whose leader had predicted a flood would destroy the U.S. West Coast. Aliens from the planet Clarion would arrive to rescue the Chosen in a flying saucer before the flood struck. Members of The Seekers quit their jobs, left their unbelieving spouses, and sold their houses and all their worldly goods in anticipation of the great day. But when the momentous day arrived – December 21, 1954 – and the flood and flying saucer failed to materialize, their leader, Dorothy Martin ("Sister Thedra") announced that her followers "had spread so much light that God had saved the world from destruction." Almost all of this cult's followers unquestioningly accepted this explanation and continued to follow her increasingly outlandish prophecies, no matter how bankrupt and destitute they now found themselves.

The People's Temple (Jonestown)- "Drinking the Kool Aid"

The mass suicide of 900 people on November 18, 1978 at Jonestown, Guyana, were not a necessary part of any prophecy or pre-existing belief system that Jim Jones, the leader of the People's Temple, had laid down for his followers. Instead, Jim Jones directed his followers to drink cyanide-laced Kool-Aid because he felt that his power over the cult was being threatened. He decided that it would be better for his followers to all die together as a community rather than to see his cult broken up. The crisis was triggered when a U.S. Court ordered Jones to return the son of two former members. However, Jones could not bring himself to do that; if he ended up surrendering, he would have effectively admitted that he did not have total power and that he would have to bow to a higher authority. Jones worried that if he complied with the court order, others would be motivated to try to get their loved ones out of his compound in Guyana, and his entire movement could collapse. So, Jones decided to poison his followers – men, women and children – rather than submit to the law or even basic concepts of human dignity.

QAnon

The far-right American political conspiracy theory and political movement known as QAnon originated in 2017, when an anonymous individual or group of individuals known as "Q" started spreading fabricated conspiracy theories online.

After spreading on 4Chan, Q's message was then amplified by more online communities and influencers. The name "Q" derives from the top security clearance issued by the United States Department of Energy (DOE) for a select few with unlimited access to highly classified government files relating to the DOE's top secret nuclear and other sensitive energy programs.[2] Q claimed to have top secret security clearance to the U.S. government's secret plans on a wide range of subjects, implying that Q was a "deep-state" insider spilling the beans. The hints that Q dropped online were referred to as "drops" or "breadcrumbs" that challenged Qanon followers to "do their own research" – consisting largely of surfing far right and fringe conspiracy websites – and finding for themselves "the truth" that Q was cryptically revealing piece by piece.

It is an established fact that if you go online and search for information on a false conspiracy theory – such as whether the 2020 presidential election was "stolen" from Trump due to massive voter fraud and manipulation by a leftist leaning Democratic political establishment and "permanent state"– you will find a disproportionate number of fringe misinformation sites that thrive on misinformation, wild conspiracy theories and anti-establishment bias. Searching for this material on social media

---

2   The "anon" in QAnon refers to any anonymous or pseudonymous person who generates internet posts. The concept of anons "doing research" and claiming to disclose otherwise classified information, while a key component of the QAnon conspiracy theory, originated from other conspiracy theory internet sites that also claimed to have special government access, such as "FBIAnon" or "CIAAnon."

is even more destructive, as algorithms developed for Facebook, YouTube, Twitter (now X), and Tik-Tok are designed to 'feed' you more of the information you display interest in. Conspiracy-related content spreads rapidly via algorithms, which introduce more and more extreme content over time to retain user interest.[3]

The most outlandish and unreality-based websites – such as The Gateway Pundit and One America News (OAN) - tend to draw the most "clicks" than their reality-based (*i.e.*, boring) competing websites because an increasing percentage of Americans feel a deep sense of alienation and distrust for "the system," so the conspiracy theories promoted by QAnon and other cult groups tend to reinforce and justify their alienation and identification with an "outsider" group such as QAnon. Thus, the internet "research" by a person who is inclined to believe conspiracy theories almost always reinforces the false premise that is being "researched."

One of QAnon's core beliefs is that a cabal of Satanic child molesters is operating a global child sex trafficking ring that is conspiring to destroy Donald J. Trump, whose political rise and election to the presidency in 2016 coincided with the emergence of this cult group. QAnon drew much of its early support from "Pizzagate," the internet conspiracy theory that Hillary Clinton and many of her key left wing and liberal supporters were involved in a secret society of child abusers and human sex traffickers being run out of Comet Ping Pong, a pizzeria in Washington, D.C. This outlandish conspiracy theory was originally spread through fake news-laden websites such as 4chan and Your News Wire. This wasn't just weirdos being weird online, though. On December 4, 2016, a gunman took the workers at Comet Ping Pong hostage while he sought out the underground child sex trafficking ring he believed was operating there. However, on the bright side, the QAnon conspiracy theorists believed that the Trump Administration was conducting a secret war against this cabal of pedophiles, and would conduct arrests and executions of thousands of cabal members on a day known as "the Storm" or "the Event."

Both the "Pizzagate" true believers, and later the faithful followers of QAnon, believed in the longstanding antisemitic trope that Jewish financier George Soros and the Rothschild family were at the center of the leftist cabal pulling the strings and levers of power both in America and

---

[3] https://www.scientificamerican.com/article/conspiracy-theories-how-social-media-can-help-them-spread-and-even-spark-violence/

around the globe. The roots of this antisemitic theory go back long before the Nazi Party adopted the notion of a worldwide Jewish conspiracy as its central plank in the 1930s, inspired by "the Protocols of the Elders of Zion," an antisemitic conspiracy pamphlet published in pre-Revolutionary Russia. The Q-update to this age-old madness argued that Soros and his ilk intended to maintain their power and influence by using liberal democratic political theories to secretly "replace" White people with black and brown people who could be more easily controlled.

The QAnon movement faced a momentary crisis when "the Storm" failed to occur and Joe Biden was declared the winner of the presidential election on November 5, 2020. However, QAnon followers were reinvigorated when Trump summoned them via a text message to Washington, D.C. for a rally outside the White House on January 6, 2021: "BE THERE, WILL BE WILD." Trump delivered on his promise when, after working the assembled crowd into a frenzy, he directed them to march on the U.S. Capital, where Congress was in the process of certifying the election for Biden. Many of those who attacked the U.S. Capitol on January 6, 2021 wore QAnon shirts and carried QAnon-style flags.

One of the most widely viewed viral images during the January 6 attack on the Capitol was that of a shirtless, heavily tattooed Arizona man wearing a bearskin headdress with horns, and a red, white and blue painted face. He was hard to miss, even amidst the surrounding chaos. Jacob Anthony Chansley, who also goes by the name Jake Angeli and is popularly known as the "QAnon Shaman," was taken into custody Saturday, January 9, and was denied bail. He was charged with civil disorder, obstruction of an official proceeding, disorderly conduct in a restricted building, demonstrating in a Capitol building, entering a restricted building without lawful authority and violent entry and disorderly conduct on Capitol grounds. However, it does not appear that Chansley destroyed any property, injured any officers, or had the intention of capturing or assassinating any elected official. Indeed, on the day after the riot, Chansley called the FBI in Washington, telling investigators that he came to the nation's capital "at the request of the president that all 'patriots' come to D.C. on January 6, 2021." In other words, he was just a more eccentric version of the millions of intellectually-challenged Americans who – without giving it much thought or any thought at all

-were following their colorful and charismatic leader wherever he led, no matter how disastrous the consequences.

We must learn to communicate with the QAnon cult members and other easily manipulated "crazies" on the political fringes before it is too late. Read on to see how it can be done.

Chapter 4

THE MAGA CULT

Donald J. Trump's legion of devoted followers is a political, social and cultural phenomenon that appears to be unique in modern American history. To be sure, John F. Kennedy, his brother Bobby Kennedy, Bill Clinton and other charismatic political figures have sparked rapturous devotion among their political followers, but the MAGA cult is something quite different from American political norms and more akin to celebrity-worship or circuit-riding preachers. As Trump himself famously bragged, he could shoot someone in broad daylight on Fifth Avenue in New York and no one would stop him. In other words, the Trump faithful believe that he can do no wrong and should not be held accountable for his actions, no matter how reprehensible. Perhaps they think him incapable of reprehensible actions, or believe that he serves a higher purpose and works in mysterious ways. No matter the reason for this blind faith, Trumpism bears the hallmarks of a cult, not a democratic political movement.

Not coincidentally, Trump's favorite collection of speeches is that of another charismatic cult leader who led Germany to its destruction during the 1930s and 1940s. While appearing on the Morning Show in March 2017, Republican political strategist Steve Schmidt mentioned that Trump kept a copy of Adolf Hitler speeches on his nightstand.[1] This confirmed what Trump's first wife, Ivana, was quoted as saying in a 1990 Vanity Fair article, which was that Trump owned a copy of "My New Order" – a printed collection of the Nazi leader's speeches.[2]

The similarity between these two cult leaders is remarkable. Hitler was unquestionably one of the most masterful propagandists of the modern era. He had millions of Nazi cult followers convinced that whatever he said must be true, and whatever he told them to do, they would do.

---

1   Benjamin Kentish@BenKentish, Monday 20 March 2017
https://thehill.com/homenews/media/394130-schmidt-trumps-only-affinity-for-reading-anything-were-the-adolf-hitler/
2   Maria Brenner, Vanity Fair

Like Trump, Hitler never took responsibility for any defeat or any even bad news. When things did not go his way, Hitler just portrayed himself and his followers as victims of a dark conspiracy. Hitler sold the German people on the totally fanciful theory that Germany's defeat in World War I was not "legitimate," but, rather, that Germany had been "stabbed in the back" by a Jewish-led cabal, and that the Jews plotted to replace the German "Aryan" people with eugenically inferior Slavic and Jewish peoples. This is ironic since the historical Aryan people were from India and bore no real relation to Germany, let alone Hitler's vision of blonde-haired, blue-eyed racial "supermen."

After the 2020 election, Trump's response could have been taken directly from Hitler's playbook: he did not lose the election legitimately; rather, it was "stolen" from him. Most of his followers, like the German people in the 1930s, ignored the uncomfortable truth and embraced the much more comforting alternative theory being offered by their Supreme Leader. In fact, 64% of the 74 million people that had voted for Trump believed that he was the victim of voter fraud and that Joe Biden was not the legitimate president. When Trump was confronted by the media with the bleak reality that he had lost the election fair and square, his answer was to label it "Fake News." Trump did not come up with this term by himself. It he directly borrowed it from Hitler's playbook, who used the German word for fake news, *Lügenpresse*, which directly translates to "the lying press".

Given that the facts regarding the 2020 election results did not support Trump's "stolen election" theory, Trump's die-hard followers were holding onto what could only be deemed a quasi-religious cult, with Trump as their cult leader. The MAGA hat and tee-shirt became the symbol of their movement, just as the swastika served as the rallying banner in pre-World War II Germany.

Like every other cult, the faith of true believers is rarely shaken when events do not work out as prophesized. Just as Trump urged his follows to march on the Capitol to "take back our democracy" from the members of Congress who had the audacity to certify the winner of the election based on the legitimate state electoral slates presented to them. Trump told them "…you'll never take back our country with weakness. You have to show strength and you have to be strong." The Trump faithful dutifully marched on the Capitol and succeeded in momentarily taking control of much of it, disrupting and delaying the Congressional proceedings, but in the end, failing to prevent the final vote that certified Joe Biden as the next president of the United States.

Nor have subsequent events served to shake the faith of most of the MAGA faithful – not the prosecutions and convictions of the Capitol insurrectionists, not the indictment and criminal conviction of Trump himself, and not even Trump's dark pronouncements as to the retribution and reign of terror that he plans to unleash on "Day One" of his second administration.

Trump's willingness to sacrifice the lives of his followers during the coronavirus pandemic was not completely dissimilar to the decision that Jim Jones made in Guyana. This was an especially perverse position for Trump, given that Republican voters skew elderly and the most important risk factor for COVID is age. The coronavirus was perceived by Trump as a threat to his power and is presidency, so he decided to hold a series of rallies throughout the U.S., despite the legitimate concerns of many advisers that they would turn into coronavirus "superspreader" events.

The first major rally was held on Saturday, June 20, 2020 at the BOK Center in Tulsa, Oklahoma, where thousands of the MAGA faithful showed up, sitting in close proximity to each other in defiance of municipal laws (and common sense) requiring "social distancing." Few of those attending even bothered to wear surgical masks, even though a vaccine for coronavirus was still not publicly available, and the mortality rate for those who were infected by the virus was still fairly high.

Herman Cain, a former Republican presidential contender, attended the rally without a mask and, from photographs and media coverage, appeared to be enjoying himself immensely with a group of friends. He tested positive for the virus days later and died shortly thereafter. A study by Stanford University economists in October 2020 revealed that the 18 rallies held by then President Trump between June 20 and September 30, 2020, likely caused 30,000 coronavirus infections and more than 700 deaths.

According to some notable psychological research studies,[3] the brains of Trump supporters are – generally speaking – wired quite differently from those of non-Trump supporters. The major psychological attributes that help explain the Trump political phenomenon can be described as follows:

---

3   See, e.g., Pettigrew, T. F. (2017). Social psychological perspectives on Trump supporters. *Journal of Social and Political Psychology, 5*(1), 107–116. https://doi.org/10.5964/jspp.v5i1.750

1. Authoritarianism

The Authoritarian personality refers to those who advocate enforcement of strict obedience to authority at the expense of personal freedom. This characteristic is commonly associated with a lack of concern for the opinions or needs of others. Authoritarian personality syndrome is a state of mind that is characterized by belief in total and complete obedience to one's authority. Those with the syndrome often display aggression toward outgroup members, submissiveness to authority, resistance to new experiences, and a rigidly hierarchical view of society. The syndrome is often triggered by fear, making it easy for leaders who exaggerate threat or fear monger to gain their allegiance.

Authoritarian personality disorders are most prevalent among right wing parties around the world. That's not to say it cannot exist on the political left: just look at Stalin or Pol Pot. In the contemporary U.S. context, this is best exemplified President Trump's speeches, which include fear-mongering about "American carnage" and vicious, absolutist terms like "losers" and "complete disasters," which are naturally appealing to those who prefer authoritarianism. While research showed that Republican voters in the U.S. scored higher than Democrats on measures of authoritarianism before Trump emerged on the political scene, a 2016 Politico survey found that people with authoritarian-leaning personalities greatly favored then-candidate Trump, which led to a correct prediction that he would win the election, despite the polls saying otherwise.

2. Social Dominance Orientation

Social dominance orientation (SDO) refers to people who have a preference for the societal hierarchy of groups, specifically with a structure in which the high-status groups have dominance over the low-status ones. Those with SDO are typically dominant, tough-minded, and driven exclusively by self-interest. "Altruism" and "empathy" are not in their vocabulary.

In Trump's speeches, he appeals to those with SDO by repeatedly making a clear distinction between groups that have a generally higher status in society (e.g., White People), and those groups that are typically thought of as belonging to a lower status (immigrants and minorities). A 2016 survey study of 406 American adults published in the journal, *Personality and Individual Differences,* found that those who scored high on both SDO and authoritarianism were also likelier to intend to vote for Trump in the election.

3. Prejudice

While not all of Trump's supporters have prejudice against ethnic and religious minorities, many do. It is a well-known fact that the Republican Party, going at least as far back to Richard Nixon's "southern strategy," used strategies that directly appealed to bigotry, such as by delivering speeches with "dog whistles"—code words and euphemisms which might appear harmless or banal, but are in fact frequently used by racists to act as a "wink" and signal prejudice toward minorities. Examples of dog whistles are Reagan's "welfare queen" attack on single black mothers, or the prolific use of the number 88 by neo-Nazis (H is the 8th letter of the alphabet and 88 can be transcribed to HH or "Heil Hitler").

While the dog whistles of the past were more subtle, Trump's are more direct. Aside from routine appeals to bigoted supporters when he calls Muslims "dangerous" and Mexican immigrants "rapists" and "murderers," one can't help but wonder what exactly he means when he says "Make America Great Again", considering the how much of American history is steeped in injustices to Black, Brown, and Native Americans.

4. Lack of Intergroup Contact

Intergroup contact refers to contact with members of groups that are outside one's own, which has been shown to reduce prejudice. Unsurprisingly, Trump's (mostly) white supporters have experienced significantly less contact with minorities than other Americans. For example, a 2016 study found that "…the racial and ethnic isolation of Whites at the zip-code level is one of the strongest predictors of Trump support." [4] Researchers further found that support for Trump increased with the voters' physical distance from the Mexican border.

5. Perceived Deprivation

Perceived deprivation refers to the experience of being deprived of something to which one believes they are entitled. It is the discontent felt when one compares their position in life to others who they feel are equal or

---

[4] Rothwell and Diego-Rosell (2016, p. 14); "Social Psychological Perspectives on Trump Supporters," Journal of Social and Political Psychologyhttps://jspp.psychopen.eu › jspp › article › view

inferior but have unfairly had more success than them. As far back as the 18th century enlightenment, this psychological phenomenon has been understood as a fundamental issue for democratic politics, For instance, Jean-Jacques Rousseau argued that the tendency to compare ourselves to those around us is the greatest barrier to harmonious coexistence, because it constantly inflames jealousy, squabbling, and petty feuds while distracting us from the common good.

Common explanations for Trump's popularity among non-bigoted voters involve economics. There is no doubt that some Trump supporters are simply angry that American jobs are being "lost" to Mexico and China, while ignoring other contributing factors, such the fact that many American jobs are disappearing due to the accelerating pace of automation. It is important to note that while this "deprivation" is perceived, and seems real to the person experiencing it, they may not be – by any objective metric – experiencing actual deprivation. In many cases, the perceived deprivation is based on an inflated sense of entitlement, such as the belief that a person is entitled to a higher salary than their job actually warrants. For example, an analysis conducted by FiveThirtyEight estimated that the median annual income of Trump supporters was $72,000, which is substantially above the average annual salaries in the U.S. in 2024, which is $59,228 per year.

Trump supporters may not be deprived in absolute terms, but it is perceptions that count when it comes to politics and voting patterns.

6. The Dunning-Kruger Effect

While relatively low IQs and the difficulty of (or inability to) logically and rationally process information are, no doubt, major factors at play among the Trump faithful, being under-informed or ignorant about the issues facing the country is only a partial explanation for the Trump phenomenon. When Trump tells them without any factual basis – that crime is skyrocketing in the United States, or that the economy is the worst it's ever been, his MAGA cult followers uncritically and completely take his word for it.

The Dunning-Kruger effect explains that the problem isn't just that diehard Trump believers are misinformed; it's that they believe they're far better informed than they really are. In other words, when presented with facts that completely refute the Trump "flat earth" world view, MAGA cult member just ignore or reject them, on the basis that they already "know" what's true and do not need to modify their worldview.

Numerous studies have shown that people who lack expertise in some area of knowledge often have a cognitive bias that prevents them from realizing that they lack expertise. This is just as true for MAGA political cult followers as it is for gun owners who don't know the first thing about gun safety but erroneously feel that they can leave guns and ammunition around the house that is readily accessible to their kids. In other words, they're not smart enough to realize they're politically naïve or dumb.

The most dangerous point for this intellectual hubris is when you've done just a little bit of research on a topic, which is enough to make you feel expert without having experienced the limits of your knowledge. Think of this as the "teenager effect", where a highschooler watches one documentary and believes they now know everything about a complex topic. This is happening on a national-scale, with Trumpers "doing their own research" into COVID, QAnon, and immigration—with disastrous results for U.S. politics.

7. Hypersensitivity to Threat

Scientific research has conclusively shown that the conservative brain has an exaggerated fear response when faced with stimuli that may be perceived as threatening. A 2008 study in the journal, *Science,* found that conservatives have a stronger physiological reaction to startling noises and graphic images compared to liberals. The National Institutes of Health reported that a brain imaging study revealed that those who lean right politically tend to have a larger amygdala — a structure that is electrically active during states of fear and anxiety.[5] And a 2014 MRI study found that it is possible to predict whether someone is a liberal or conservative simply by looking at their brain activity while they view threatening images.[6] Specifically, the brains of self-identified conservatives generated more activity overall in response to the threatening images.

Clearly, then, the brain responses of the MAGA faithful are automatic. They do not think about politics long enough to be properly influenced by logic or reason. As long as Trump continues his fear mongering by

---

5 National Institutes of Health (NIH) (.gov) https://www.ncbi.nlm.nih.gov › articles › PMC5793824 by WS Pedersen · 2018
6 Political Orientations Are Correlated with Brain Structure in ...National Institutes of Health (NIH) (.gov)https://www.ncbi.nlm.nih.gov › articles › PMC3092984 by R Kanai · 2011

constantly portraying Muslims and Mexican immigrants as imminent dangers, conservative brains will involuntarily light up, keeping his followers energized and focused on their own safety and that of their families. With Trump as their protector, their allegiance is pledged to him unconditionally.

8. Terror Management Theory

The social psychological theory of "Terror Management" explains why Trump's fear mongering is so effective. The theory is based on the fact that humans, who have an awareness of the inevitability of their own mortality, have an existential terror and anxiety that can be "managed" through religion, political ideologies, and national identities. These beliefs and identities provide a buffer for the individual, instilling life with meaning and value. When confronted with a fearful event – real or imagined – people tend to defend those who share the same worldview as them, whether it be national or ethnic identity, and act more aggressively towards those who are perceived as threatening that worldview. In particular, numerous studies have shown that when people are reminded of death or danger of death, their voting habits veer decidedly to the right, favoring more conservative candidates.

Chapter 5

HOW SOCIAL MEDIA HAS ACCELERATED THE "DUMBING DOWN" OF AMERICA

According to social psychologist Jonathan Haidt, the rise of social media platforms - such as Facebook, Twitter and YouTube - over the past ten years has accelerated the "dumbing down" of Americans and our core institutions.[1] Haidt has explained that social media has made it easier for people to intimidate others who might dissent or question their views, such that many people have stopped expressing their opinions in media outlets or social media platforms because they realistically fear that they may be subjected to a campaign of retaliation and character assassination.[2] Online interactions take place without face-to-face contact, producing what psychologist Suler calls the "online disinhibition effect".[3] Put simply, when people feel anonymous, physically alone, and unaccountable for their words and actions, people do and say things that they otherwise wouldn't. Just compare the extreme and hostile opinions voiced in the comment sections of news on social media to the discussions you have with strangers or even friends in public and in real life.

The effect of social media is that people with differing viewpoints no longer engage in legitimate discussion over issues; instead, they retreat to the safety of their Blue or Red media outlets and social media websites where they can express their opinions in relative safety. This is further amplified by the game-like nature of "reaction" buttons to online comments, which trigger a dopamine rush for commenters and typically reward the most outrageous ideas. Thus, without any reasoned and respectful public debate or discussion of very real issues, the ability of Americans to engage in critical thinking and debate has been largely lost. As with the tower of

---

1 nz.co.nz/national/programmes/sunday/audio/2018845545/the-reason-why-america-has-become-uniquely-stupid#:~:te
2 https://www.theatlantic.com/magazine/archive/2022/05/social-media-democracy-trust-babel/629369/
3 https://pubmed.ncbi.nlm.nih.gov/15257832/

Babel in the Book of Genesis, the people have lost the ability to understand and communicate with one another. This is fatal to both intellectual development and the proper functioning of democratic institutions.

* * *

This deterioration in the ability of Americans to communicate with one another happened fairly quickly. We proudly elected the country's first Black president in November 2008, legalized gay marriage in many states, enacted the Affordable Care Act (Obamacare) giving access to proper health care to millions of Americans who previously could not afford health insurance, and seemed to be on a progressive trajectory on many other issues. And throughout the world, democracy seemed to be finally gaining the upper hand over the forces of tyranny. Arab Spring brought a form of democracy to some Arab states, while tearing apart others, such as Syria.

And then Social Media gained dominance, rewarding hateful and angry soundbites over any rational discourse or debate on important issues. In 2005, only 5% of US adults used any social media; by 2019, 79% were active social media users.[4] The penetration of social media use is tremendous, with young people especially active online. According to the Pew Research Center, here are the top social media platforms used by young adults ages 18–29:

- YouTube: 95%
- Instagram: 71%
- Facebook: 70%
- Snapchat: 65%
- TikTok: 48%

With limited exceptions of some media outlets with limited audiences – such as PBS – ratings for TV news became increasingly driven through copycat strategies based on online content, with a maximization of outrage and angry denunciations which required the marginalization of anything resembling reasoned debate or dissent. Even our educational institutions and academic institutions have been paralyzed with political

---

4   https://www.google.com/search?client=safari&rls=en&q=US+social+media+use+percentage+over+time&ie=UTF-8&oe=UTF-8

polarization, with the Israeli-Hamas war turning some student factions violently against others based upon ethnic, religious and political differences.

Haidt is a proponent of the cyclical theory of history, which originated with the ancient Greeks and was picked up by Muslim scholars in the 14th and 15th centuries. The theory is that history repeats itself in 80 to 100 year cycles, which is the span of about four generations. For America, generation 1 would be that of our Founding Fathers, who masterminded our democracy (actually democratic republic, a crucial difference) by designing three branches of government with checks and balances to ensure (or at least stave off) the inevitable rise of populist demagogues and tyrannical governments that often followed democratic experiments throughout history, notably in both Athens and the Roman Republic.

The same cycle can be seen with many family-owned companies. The founder is a hardworking visionary who builds the company from scratch, using a combination of intelligence, perseverance and "never give up" attitude to accomplish his or her goals. But then the second and third generations, raised in greater comfort and security than the founder, inevitably grow soft and lazy, resulting in the decline of the business and financial insecurity for the fourth generation. Either the company goes bust and the fourth generation has to start building something from scratch to be successful, or they retrench what remains of the company and rebuild it back into a successful operation, if they are so fortunate to do so.

According to Rishabh Bhardwaj, Knowledge Manager at Genpact, social media is killing our ability to think by creating a false sense of connection and encouraging people to share their thoughts and feelings without any filter or thought-process involved.[5] The tendency of people using social media is that they are compelled to share everything about their thoughts and feelings. Ironically, this tends to leave people feeling overwhelmed, anxious, and even more lonely that when they started "sharing." The endless pursuit of "likes" and "followers" creates social media addicts who keep spending (some might say *wasting*) more and more on time chasing imaginary rabbits down the hole. It has gotten to the point where people are losing their ability to interact with people in the real world, especially with those who might be different from us. On social media, we can safely navigate cyberspace with those who look and

---

5   https://www.linkedin.com/pulse/social-media-killing-human-tendency-think-rishabh-bhardwaj#:~:text=

think like us, in a kind of echo chamber where our preconceptions and beliefs are reinforced, never challenged. It has also created an environment of instant gratification, with no waiting for feedback or positive reinforcement from others. The "reality principle" – a concept first articulated by Freud, refers to the mind's ability to assess the reality of the external world and act upon it accordingly, as opposed to acting solely based on immediate pleasure gratification – no longer applies to many heavy social media users. The "external world" has been reduced as far as possible, making the "real world" of the internet and social media user glued to his or her device most waking hours the only reality that they understand or want to inhabit.

There is growing evidence that social media is both psychologically and physically addictive. Social media is a form of persuasive technology, as are smartphones or slot machines at casinos. The godfather of persuasive technology, psychologist B.J. Fogg, who resides in Palo Alto, California, is affiliated with the Stanford Persuasive Technology Lab, a lab purposely built to produce machines designed to change human behavior. Persuasive technology and design, fundamentally, is about creating digital environments that modify certain parts of a user's psyche better than the real-world equivalent does.[6] Socializing via Instagram translates into the exchange of likes and comments, which is simple to understand, quantifiable, and very satisfying—at least in the short term. When receiving feedback like "likes" or comments, the neurotransmitter Dopamine, a "feel good chemical," is triggered in your brain, which then plays a role as a "reward center" for your body, providing positive feelings of well-being through increased motivation, a better mood, and greater attention. By contrast, real-life human interactions are complex and ambiguous, rarely straightforward, and can leave us confused. Navigating the ambiguity of face-to-face interactions requires social acumen, whereas understanding your position in the social media hierarchy is as simple as counting your followers.

The success of persuasive technology on social media platforms flows from three primary factors: motivation, ability and triggers. When talking about social media; the "motivator" of the user is social acceptance and the desire to avoid being socially rejected; the "ability" is the ease of use of the app; and the "triggers" are notifications and news feeds. What this

---

[6] https://tedxsydney.com/idea/is-social-media-destroying-humankind/#:

means is the simplicity of persuasive design, while demanding constant attention, has the power to definitively change human behavior.[7] Social media applications are designed to keep users returning without the use of advertisements or branded content as in the early days of advertising. The social media user of today is primarily influenced by interaction with and acceptance from other users. Advertising merely exploits the attention you're already giving to online platforms. The TikTok algorithm, for example, is specifically designed to influence young people's worldview. From the moment you create an account, the user is bombarded with fine-tuned messaging, making it virtually impossible for the user to resist the urge to return time and time again until he or she is totally hooked.

Ramsay Brown, the founder of Dopamine Labs in Los Angeles, ominously reports: "We have now developed a rigorous technology of the human mind, and that is both exciting and terrifying. We have the ability to twiddle some knobs in a machine learning dashboard we build, and around the world, hundreds of thousands of people are going to quietly change their behavior in ways that, unbeknownst to them, feel second-nature but are really by design."[8]

* * *

It is unsurprising that social media addiction is one of the fastest growing mental illnesses among young people in America. That is the intended goal of these platforms in the first place. For many young people, checking social media is the first thing they do when they wake up in the morning. And it's the last thing they do at night. Research shows that 16- to 24-year-olds spend an average of three hours a day using social media. This is true even as increasing numbers of people sense that their habits are not healthy for them.[9]

The U.S. Surgeon General issued a 2023 advisory report entitled Social Media and Youth Mental Health, outlining the scientific evidence regarding social media's negative effects on youth mental health, finding it to be widespread and pervasive.[10] It found that social media platforms

---

7   Id.
8   https://tedxsydney.com/idea/is-social-media-destroying-humankind/
9   https://www.newportinstitute.com/resources/co-occurring-disorders/social-media-addiction/?utm_source=google&utm
10 https://www.aecf.org/blog/social-medias-concerning-effect-on-teen-mental-health?gad_source=1&gclid

were little more than "clickbait" designed to draw young users into their digital web, absorbing as much of their daily attention as possible.

It is very easy for young people to become addicted to social media. The social media platforms are deliberately designed to overwhelm the user's self-control. Bottomless pages offer no natural stopping points and invite endless scrolling. Persistent cues, such as notifications and reminders, grab the user's attention when it drifts. Some features (bright colors, stimulating rings and dings) mimic the hypnotic flow of slot machines, which for decades has proven to be an especially profitable mode for casinos.

But perhaps the most powerful force behind social media addiction is its appeal to our innate social instincts.[11] Social media directly plays into the insecurities that all of us feel, but particularly adolescents who are just finding their way in the world and searching for the proper launch pad into adulthood. Just as people with extreme insecurity may seek a place of belonging in a cult group, social media manipulates one's sense of insecurity and low esteem by directly appealing to our innate psychological need for a sense of belonging.

Among the many other negative impacts of social media addiction is that it leads to poor concentration and memory due to frequent shifts in focus. There is a clinical name for this: "brain rot." The brain, and in particular its ability to reason and to remember things, deteriorates. So no wonder that social media addicts may appear to – and act – stupid.

---

11 Id.

Chapter 6

HOW TO TALK TO A TRUMP SUPPORTER

The cardinal rule when you find yourself in the presence of Trump supporter is NOT to talk about politics. Your conversation should revolve around (1) the weather (but avoid drawing any connections between the extreme weather patterns your area has been experiencing with Climate Change), (2) sports (but avoid mentioning the Kansas Chiefs football player who is dating Taylor Swift), or (3) music (as long as it is Country and Western, and has nothing to do with Taylor Swift).

Most importantly, it is important to avoid "trigger" words that can upset the Trump supporter, who is typically delicate as a snowflake, and most likely an older white man who is generally disappointed with his life, filled with grievances real and imagined, and would like to avoid taking personal responsibility for bad life decisions.

Here are some words to avoid at all costs:
- Racism
- Sexism
- Misogyny (although he probably won't know what it means)
- Bigotry
- Diversity
- Minority representation
- People of color
- Black Lives Matter
- Black people
- Immigrants, refugees, asylum seekers (or another other words that would apply to most Trump supporters' ancestors when they arrived in the U.S.)
- The Broadway Show: *Hamilton*
- Rights (unless preceded by "gun")
- *New York Times*

- Islamophobia
- Hispanic
- Whitewashing
- Greenwashing
- Brunch
- Implicit bias
- Toxic masculinity
- Transgender or Drag
- LGBTQ
- Multi-family housing
- California
- White Privilege
- Microaggression
- Climate Change
- Feminism
- Women
- The Clintons
- The Obamas
- Kamala Harris or Tim Walz

ICE BREAKERS

One good strategy for easing into a conversation that has nothing to do with the weather or sports is to comment that Biden is too old and infirm to survive another term as President, and that it was the right thing to do for him to have bowed out of the presidential race. Refer to this as clear evidence of "Elder Abuse," which should get a sympathetic response from your MAGA companion, and leading him to believe that you are "one of them."

You may then cautiously suggest that Trump too is "losing it" and that it may not be a wise idea for the American public to let him get his finger back on the nuclear button, or do something foolish like handing Ukraine and maybe Poland or the Baltic states over to Putin. Ok, yes, prices are too high but the economy is strong and things could get a lot worse under Trump if the extremists surrounding him were given a serious chance to implement Agenda 2025, cut taxes any deeper, or whatever the Heritage Foundation is calling their plan to dismantle the Education

Department and other parts of the federal agencies that we rely upon to protect the environment and countless other governmental tasks that we take for granted. After all, don't we want a balanced budget, strong allies, and a healthy country?

This is no time for a right-wing revolution, you should quietly argue, while giving him the empathetic vibes he so craves.

EPILOGUE: MAKING AMERICA SANE AGAIN

Perhaps I am being excessively nostalgic, but when I look back to my younger days (many, many years ago) while growing up in a small town of 20,000 people just north of New York City (Pelham), it seemed that a sense of honor, respect for the concepts of truth and fairness, respect for one's neighbor, and love and pride in one's community and country were never in question. It was just part of our DNA as Americans. Of course, on election day every November, there were Republicans and Democrats competing against each other for the same office, from the local level to – every four years – for President of the United States, but there was never a sense that the political opposition was somehow evil or "un-American." There were differences of opinion on a wide range of subjects, to the economy, national debt, defense spending, and whether we should put fluoride in our drinking water. But first and foremost, we were all Americans with an unspoken but unwavering love of our country, our freedoms, and our democratic institutions. Any disputes we had were family disputes within the American family. There was much more than bound us together than that which divided us.

My family was a staunch Irish-American Catholic family of Democrats. My grandfather was a motorman with the New York City Transit Authority, and my uncle was an organizer with the International Longshoremen's Union (ILA). They often regaled us with stories of working men and women fighting for their right to fair wages by walking on union picket lines, and the pitched battles with Pinkerton guards and non-union "scab" workers that companies hired in order to keep the unions from organizing their workers and representing their interests. But by the post-World War II period, during the 1950s and 1950s, the right of working people to organize had been pretty well established, and both the middle and working classes, as well as corporate America and their shareholders, experienced sustained and unparalleled growth and success. Anything and everything seemed possible, and it was generally assumed that each generation of Americans would do better than the ones that preceded them. There was a peaceful transfer of presidential power in Washington, D.C., every four or eight years, with the idea that an incumbent president who had lost the election would try to hang onto power by claiming that the election was "stolen" from him so improbable that even Hollywood studios shied away from the idea as too much like science fiction. Both Democratic and Republican candidates owed their allegiance first to the U.S. Constitution and the three co-equal branches of government that had operated reasonably well to keep the wheels of our democracy churning along. After all, we were not some unstable banana republic or third-world dictatorship where the party or strongman in power held onto that power at all costs. We were so much better than that. We were the beacon of truth, justice and democracy that set the gold standard for how people in a diverse society can come together, work together, and peacefully resolve their differences within the frame of law and their democratic institutions.

To be sure, the country still suffered from the lingering effects of the "original sin" of slavery, but the Civil Rights movement and the enactment of the Civil Rights Act of 1964 under the bold leadership of President Lyndon B. Johnson did much to lay the groundwork for the elimination – or at least significant reduction – of racial discrimination in the country. I myself and the rest of my family participated in numerous marches and demonstrations in support of equal rights for African-American, and one of our Pelham Memorial High School fellow students, Michael "Mickey" Schwerner, was one of the three civil rights workers who were tragically killed in rural Neshoba County, Mississippi on June 21, 1964. The assassinations of Dr. Martin Luther King, Jr., and then Robert Kennedy led to several days of rage in inner city neighborhoods across the country, but by and large, the American people still believed in and trusted in their democratic institutions and the Rule of Law, despite serious remaining issues of racial, economic and environmental justice throughout the country. Even those who protested America's continuing involvement in the Vietnam War and its escalation, such as myself, strongly believed that our right to protest, and to express our political views and opposition to the War, was a cherished right under the U.S. Constitution and that if those rights – or American democracy and national security – were truly in jeopardize, we would be the first to fight and, if necessary, die to protect those rights.

Under President Johnson, the U.S. also embarked on the most ambitious program since the New Deal to tackle the problem of systemic poverty that trapped one generation of poor people after another in the grinding and soul-wrenching cycle of poverty. Called the War on Poverty, numerous Great Society programs led me and many other idealistic young men and women to join VISTA, the Peace Corp. and other programs that brought us together with farm workers in California and housing project residents in the cities, all of whom were fighting to participate in America's economic mainstream and to earn a ticket to the American middle-class dream of economic security, a college education, and even home ownership. I had the honor of working with Caesar Chavez, President of the United Farm Workers (UFW) in organizing grape and other produce workers in California and Oregon, and also lived and worked in the housing projects operated by the Seattle Housing Authority. Some of my fellow organizers were raised, like myself, in middle-class families, and others came from more challenging backgrounds, but we all felt the same sense of purpose and pride that we were helping build a better and more equitable America, where every American would have the opportunity to get a good education and a good job, as part of our American birthright.

Even as recent as the 9/11 terrorist attacks, Americans set aside their differences and were united as one, standing shoulder to shoulder to recommit ourselves to protecting and rebuilding America and its democratic spirit. But then something deeply troubling happened. Our country drifted into two camps – one Blue and one Red. The cable news channels and Social Media accelerated this divisive trend when it became apparent that there were larger audiences and more attention paid to extreme and antagonistic views. While voices of moderation had once dominated the T.V. and radio airwaves, insults, lies and denunciations quickly became the order of the day. Few commentators and "talking heads" were actually engaging in reasonable discussion with each other. The ratings went up when people were screaming at each other or propounding totally unsubstantiated half-truths and outright lies. It got so bad that most Americans retreated into their "news silos," with Blue Democrats seeking solace by watching MSNBC, with an occasional visit to CNN, which Red MAGA Republicans flocked to the Fox New channel, and then when Fox News was unwilling to drink the continuous toxic flow of Trump/MAGA Kool Aid, they followed Trump to his "Truth Social" ap.

So, what to do? How do we reverse this dangerous trend towards "irreconcilable differences" between Blue and Red America. Is a political divorce inevitable or can we overcome our differences by collectively realizing that we have an extraordinary political system in place that desperately needs the support of all of us if it is to continue to survive.

The first place to start is with a re-commitment of our educational system – both for our children as well as our adults – to social studies and American history, so that every man, woman and child in this country is fully familiar with the basic provisions of our U.S. Constitution, our electoral system and how the three branches of our government work together, and sometimes in competition with each other, to ensure that the masterful system of "checks and balances" designed by our Founders, continues to work for all Americans. During the New Deal era under President Franklin D. Roosevelt, it was realized that the country's economic challenges (and near collapse) were exacerbated by the lack of basic knowledge by many Americans as to how our system of government really worked, which led to low civic engagement. The government responded with ambitious adult education programs that not only produced more knowledgeable citizens, but tended to draw them into the civic and political system as active participants, or even just as voters.[1] Many of our newly sworn U.S. citizens have a better grasp of our political processes and institutions than native-born Americans since they are required to know at least the most important details of the political system of the country that they are joining.

It is also time for Social Media platforms to assume greater public responsibility by hosting more educational and civic-based content to drive up citizen participation in our democratic processes. If this is not done voluntarily, then some government mandate is long overdue. Our streets and highways are subject to strict traffic laws to ensure public safety, and so similar guardrails and guidelines should be in place for those media companies profiting from the internet and digital highways have become an essential part of the lives of virtually all Americans.

In our schools, the bans and restrictions on the use of cell phones by students during school hours is being adopted by schools across the

---

1   https://newprairiepress.org/cgi/viewcontent.cgi?article=2011&context=aerc).

nation, and will inevitably lead to a better learning environment for our students. The need for boundaries to be set between online and offline activities by students is long overdue, and restricted cell phone use will also result in a reduction of cyberbullying or other forms of online harassment and abuse:

The U.S. Surgeon General's 2023 advisory report, Social Media and Youth Mental Health, recommends actions to be taken by policymakers, technology companies, parents and others to ensure the online safety of young people.[2]

What Parents and Caregivers can do.

Parents and caregivers are encouraged to create a family media plan to help establish healthy technology boundaries at home, including social media use. "Tech free zones" in the house, such as at the kitchen or dining room table, can also be established, and "in-person" tech-free interpersonal relationships should be encouraged, which often leads to real friendships (something sorely lacking in today's digital dependent world).

What technology companies can do:

1. Conduct and facilitate transparent and independent assessments of the impact of social media products and services on children and adolescents.

2. Prioritize user health and safety in the design and development of social media products and services.

3. Design, develop, and evaluate platforms, products, and tools that foster safe and healthy online environments for youth.

4. Share data relevant to the health impact of platforms and strategies employed to ensure safety and wellbeing with independent researchers and the public in a manner that is timely and protects privacy.

---

2   https://www.aecf.org/blog/social-medias-concerning-effect-on-teen-mental-health?gad_source=1&gclid

5. Create effective and timely systems and processes to adjudicate requests and complaints from young people, families, educators, and others to address online abuse, harmful content and interactions, and other threats to children's and adolescents' health and safety.

What Policymakers can do:

1. Strengthen protections to ensure greater safety for children and adolescents interacting with all social media platforms, by:

    a) Developing age-appropriate health and safety standards for technology platforms.

    b) Require a higher standard of data privacy for children and adolescents.

    c) Pursue policies that further limit access—in ways that minimize the risk of harm—to social media for all children and adolescents.

2. Ensure technology companies share data relevant to the health impact of their platforms with independent researchers and the public in a manner that is timely, sufficiently detailed, and protects privacy.

3. Support the development, implementation, and evaluation of digital and media literacy curricula in schools and within academic standards.

4. Support increased funding for future research on the benefits and harms of social media use.

5. Engage with international partners working to protect children and adolescents against online harm to their health and safety.

What Researchers can do:

1. Establish the impact of social media on youth mental health as a research priority and develop a shared research agenda.

2. Develop and establish standardized definitions and measures for social media and mental health outcomes that are regularly evaluated and applied across research contexts.

3. Evaluate best practices for healthy social media use in collaboration with experts including healthcare providers, parents, and youth.

4. Enhance research coordination and collaboration.

In other words, if we can learn to control our addiction to technological devices and media platforms that trap us in narrow "information silos" that suppress any real rational discussion, and if we can perhaps even talk to one another in a respectful and reasonable manner (yes, this actually happened back in the day), then there is at least a ray of hope that we can properly address the "stupidity crisis" that is overwhelming our country.

www.ingramcontent.com/pod-product-compliance
Lightning Source LLC
Chambersburg PA
CBHW060704030426
42337CB00017B/2763